THOUGHTS
OF A
PURE
MIND

Are your thoughts pure?

CALVIN BLAND

ISBN-10: 0615780148
ISBN-13: 9780615780146

Introduction

This book was written to make you think, inspire, and open your eyes to different concepts. What seemed to be the truth might actually have been a lie. The poems found in this book are the thoughts and emotions of the author. The poetry is very deep and touching but also very fun and exciting to read. Take a journey into the author's mind and discover a whole new world. The poems in this book range from happy and uplifting to sad and depressing. Thoughts of a pure mind will guide you to start thinking about the world in a new light. This book will show you how a mind should truly function. Be prepared for a spiritual journey like no other the journey you've always been waiting for. You didn't find this book it found you. Now let the journey begin.

Table of Contents

Table of Contents

Thoughts of a pure mind

Everyone is born with a pure mind,

With thoughts as pure as rain drops from the sky,

It's the world that we live in that make our
thoughts become non pure,

They un purify our minds with fear and
propaganda to make us uncertain and unsure,

Mental warfare is now the new world war,

But you can fight back by keeping
your mind elevated,

Keep your mind elevated higher
than the Himalaya's,

We must mentally destroy this world and that's
the true apocalypse of the Mayan's,

Everyone should try to have a
mind state like Gandhi's,

Unfortunately most people have
the mindstate of a zombie,

People with pure minds must
awake the walking dead,

We must raise the vibration of
knowledge going to their heads,

So try to ignore all the negative allure,

Then once again our minds will become pure.

The

journey

now

begins!

Only God knows

They say only god knows,

But if you don't know god does it even matter?

What is god is it something
spiritual or physical matter?

Is it something you can't see or touch?

Is it a being in the sky that wants to rule over us?

Or is it a concept created by another human
being so they could get one over on us?

Maybe this whole time we've been lied to,

We've been looking for god outside of ourselves
but did you ever think god might be inside you?

I am no longer on a search for god because
I found me and maybe you
should try and find you,

I'm serving new food for thought on the menu,

It's not about what god knows because
nobody knows you better than you,

When you start to know yourself your shine
brighter than a movie star,

Now is the perfect time for us to become
who we truly are.

There's

power in

your

thoughts!

Free your mind

_____

It might be hard to free your mind in
a world where nothing is free,

But if you don't free your mind
you'll end up paying for it,

Don't just let your mind float in outer space
you've got to try and stay in orbit,

Most peoples minds are boxed in,

When really their minds should
be soaring at mach ten,

Even today's school systems
leave our minds boxed in,

Because the students can't expand their minds
beyond anything their teacher has taught them,

So we spend our whole lives
living inside of a box,

And anything outside of the box can't
be fact so we see it as fictional,

If more people thought outside of the
box we'd solve the worlds problems,

Then no longer would we be living
in misery and hatred,

WE must free our minds out of this matrix,

But most people won't see what
I'm saying even with lasik,

When we free our minds we'll be able to travel
the cosmos without the use of a spaceship,

It's about time we get away
from our mental slavery,

It's hard to free your mind
but all it takes is true bravery.

Thoughts.............

Life after or afterlife

What if when you were born you really died?

what if when you died you
were really being born?

What if your birth was truly your death?

What if your last gasp for air
was really your first breath?

Maybe physically dying will
keep you spiritually alive,

This just means even with a physical
death the spirit will still thrive,

We shouldn't look at death
in such a negative light,

We all have our own paths in life so there's no
need to put up a competitive fight,

A physical death shouldn't be such a sad time
it should be more joyous,

There should be partying laughter and
all kinds of happy noises,

Death isn't the end it's truly the beginning,

Life goes on it truly has no ending,

Only scary thing about death
is the fear of the unknown,

Understand that everything you
do in this life time matters,

The true meaning of this life is to
prepare you for the life after.

Your thoughts
will turn into
your reality!

Sweet nothingness

_____

Even if you have nothing,

That still means you have something,

I call it the sweet nothingness,

That's because even nothing has to
have a place to exist,

You can't get something from nothing,

But nothing can turn into something,

This means even if you were born with nothing
you can still become something,

You can go from being homeless to
living in a mansion,

Just open up your mind and leave room
for expansion,

Even true love can happen in the most
craziest circumstances,

It may start out as nothing then turn
into something,

This is really love in it's purest form,

Everything starts out as nothing this is even
how the universe was formed,

Building from nothing just gives you
a point to start from,

Just have belief in yourself and follow the
beat of your hearts drum.

"Pure thoughts

will make

a pure heart"

Depression

_____

Sometimes I can't run away from my
deep depression,

Sometimes I can't stop the dark thoughts
from manifesting,

How can I get the world to love me when
sometimes I don't even like me,

These are the thoughts I have when the
depression takes over my psyche,

When you want to be left alone and don't
want anyone near you,

When you push away friends and loved ones
because they become too fearful,

Then you wonder if life is even worth living,

I start to lose my focus,

I Start to feel worthless non motivated
and hopeless,

I might look happy but looks can be deceiving,

Smiling on the outside but on the
inside I'm grieving,

Do you know how it feels to cry
yourself to sleep?

In my dreams is the only time I can get away,

When I'm dreaming that's the only
time I feel alive,

Every morning feels like death when
I open my eyes.

Depression

We all suffer from depression!

Blossom

Knowledge and love can help a child blossom,

Like sunlight and water to a flower,

Plant a seed in the mind of the earth and
watch it grow,

Plant the seed of knowledge into the mind
of a child and watch that child glow,

So many kids grow up lost and forgotten,

Just because a child is growing doesn't mean
they've been given a proper chance to blossom,

It's hard to blossom when you were never
planted in the right soil,

So children become dandelion's instead of roses,

And the lawn will become damaged when
dandelion's go unnoticed,

The life of a child today is hard and probably
becoming even harder,

But it could become easier on them if we all
became gardeners.

Changing your thoughts through poetry!

"All kids deserve a chance to blossom"

Thoughts...........

The underdog

_____

Teachers turned their backs on him,

They figured him to be non intelligent,

They figured him irrelevant,

Not knowing that his mind was heaven sent,

His mind expands beyond their knowledge
of knowing,

He's already been there while their still
wondering where their going,

You see them as heroes but Obama's
a liar and Romney's a crook,

The mathematics of my mind expands beyond
the pages of any geometry book,

This is what happens when the underdog
becomes an over achiever,

I use to be my only believer,

I was never given a path so I decided
to make one,

Nobody can take me off my path because
it was self created,

I use to suffer from self hatred,

Not knowing the whole time within me
was greatness,

While most people are waiting on the
world to change I can be the one crazy
enough to change it.

Thoughts of a
pure mind!

Have pure thoughts!

Sadness

Even in daylight everything seems blacked out,

It follows over me like a black cloud,

It makes me want to lash out,

It has me drinking until I pass out,

It has such a strong grip on me,

So many defeats I'm just waiting on a victory,

Life is a struggle,

Life is a puzzle,

Just hope I can fit the pieces together,

This thing called life has to get better,

While most people are out having fun and drinking,

I'm sitting in a dark room just thinking,

With a blank stare on my face no blinking,

In my own separate mindspace,

Just hoping I can find faith,

To guide me on this journey,

To help me escape from this sickness
and madness,

I guess it's safe to say I suffer from sadness.

Do you
suffer from
sadness?

Welcome to
pure thoughts

Black skin

Growing up as a child I thought it made
me inferior,

I thought it made me less of a person,

It made me feel like a burden,

When you're a child you become what other
people think of you,

When the whole world thinks you're inferior you
actually start to think it to,

For a young kid growing up this is very painful
and confusing,

As I got older I stopped listening to the rest
of the world and started to gain knowledge
for myself,

Most people don't know so I figured I'd be the one to start telling them,

I have black skin because of a hormone called melatonin,

This element is found all throughout nature and the universe,

My skin use to make me feel alone,

Now I understand and realize the whole entire universe is my home,

So all the negativity about black skin to me no longer matters,

Because now I know I come from the divine order of nature and universal matter.

Learn to love your skin!

Antichrist

I've been sent here to destroy everything
they believe in,

I'm going to expose their truth as lies,

What you see as false may actually
be the truth in disguise,

The people you see as hero's might
actually be villains,

Maybe you can learn more from a person
in jail then a politician?

Because a person behind bars knows what it
feels like to not have a pot to piss in,

They can try but nothing can stop my mission,

Not even a physical death can deter me,

My soul lives forever so nothing in this physical
world can hurt me,

They portray me as pure evil,

When really I'm a kind soul that's been
sent here to save the people,

Before you love someone you must love yourself,

So before you judge me you should
judge yourself.

Never
judge
another
person

Or you
will be
judged!

I amaze me

It's a little eerie and crazy,

When I read my poetry sometimes and even
I amaze me,

I know my poetry will lead me to great wealth
and accomplishments,

But it's just crazy how I can read my own writings
and still feel astonishment,

Sometimes I'm not sure how I can create these
great concepts,

But I know these creations will make sure my
family and my mom's set,

It's like I'm a black hole that just engulfs
information,

Then I formulate concepts in my mind from the info and put it on paper and that's an amazing sensation,

Like a river my mind flows in many directions,

It's difficult for writers block to block me because my mind is flowing in so many directions,

Plus the flowing currents of my thoughts will erode any obstacle,

It amazes me how my mind can make the impossible seem possible,

It's a very strange feeling when you start to amaze yourself,

All it takes is focus and belief and you too will begin to amaze yourself.

Always have belief in yourself!

Patience is a virtue

———————

They say patience is a virtue,

And trying to live a fast life may hurt you,

But I still must pick up the pace,

I have to keep moving forward I can't
stay in one place,

Me and success have to attract like a magnet,

I can't stand still I can't afford to be stagnant,

I have to make life better for me and
my loved ones,

All the love they have for me that's where
I get my strength from,

They say if your not given a path then you just
have to make one,

I have to make things happen and not
wait for them to occur,

I know patience is a virtue but if you wait to long
life will pass you by in a blur,

I just have to keep my vision in my minds eye,

And just try to stay patient waiting on my time.

Be
patient
and
never
give up!

Always
have
faith in
yourself!

Empty stomach

It feels as if I'm living life on an empty stomach,

With nothing to stop the hunger,

I don't want to live like this any longer,

They say what doesn't kill you only makes
you stronger,

In my mind I see glimpses of tragedy,

The world seems to be one big travesty,

Feels like god is always mad at me,

I'm searching for something to stop these
hunger pains,

All I hear is thunder and all I see is rain,

I'm searching for something to put me
in a better mood,

But the hunger that I'm feeling won't
be satisfied with food,

I want to know what it feels like to be full of life,

But instead I feel an emptiness in my
everyday plight.

Ever have
that
empty
feeling?

I know
it's not
a good
feeling

Mind travel

I mind travel to get away from the norm,

When it's cold outside I envision a place
that's warm,

When I'm sad I think of happier moments,

Mind traveling is like a drug that is very
strong and potent,

Best part is you never have to pack any luggage,

Try it once and you'll eventually start to love it,

And I don't have to stay earthbound I can even
enter different realms and dimensions,

To shelter me away from all of the negative
premonitions,

And all these harsh human conditions,

I want to get away because I really don't
like it here,

The fake happiness hatred and jealousy
I swear I don't like it here,

So I travel to a heavenly sanctuary,

Where only my inner god can hear me.

Find your

place of

happiness

When

feeling down!

10 steps ahead of you

―――――――

The things you're just now thinking about I've
already thought about and analyzed,

I know that must leave you feeling
mentally vandalized,

I'm living in the future while you're still
waiting on it,

Stuck in the past filled with jealousy and
that's why you're hating on it,

Now your life seems all messed up,

Still trying to play catch up,

Why don't you just look in the mirror and fess up,

Nobody did this to you, you did it to yourself,

Don't ever start problems you won't know
how to solve,

Approach me with the wrong mind state
and feel the wrath of god,

I'm always cool calm and collective but
my minds always been a little bit odd,

I've always been silent and quiet,

But the thoughts in my mind are loud
enough to start a riot,

The wrath of god is within me but I've
just been concealing it,

So you really just need to calm down
and understand the type of spiritual forces
you're dealing with.

Always ten steps ahead!

Thoughts........

Black love

It's very powerful and yet we still hate ourselves,

We hate our own hair and skin so we do foolish
things to recreate ourselves,

Not knowing were created from a divine essence,

And not only do we hate ourselves we
hate each other,

When really we need to gain knowledge
and teach each other,

Now I could blame society,

But why should I pay attention to them when
they've always lied to me?

All the falsehoods about black people
once even blinded me,

Were lied about in the history books,

Made to believe were nothing but slaves
and crooks,

As a child these type of lies haunted me, When
gaining knowledge for myself I learned we created the modern worlds philosophy's,

This is the perfect moment to stop hating
ourselves,

Because right now it's time for us to start
embracing ourselves.

Love is

a powerful

drug!

.........Of A pure

Everything happens for a reason

When my mom met my dad it wasn't by accident,

There were divine forces working in action,

Everything happens exactly the way it's
supposed to happen,

That includes bad and good situations,

Even when something feels so bad and
you're not going to make it,

It's to make you stronger and prepare
you for greatness,

I wrote this poem for a specific purpose,

And right now you're reading this for
a specific purpose,

It's because you're much deeper than what
appears on the surface,

So don't doubt or hate yourself because
that's self treason,

You must understand you're here for a reason,

I'm starting to find mine and you can find yours,

Don't get caught up in self created mind wars,

Because it will put up a mental barricade,

Just understand everything happens for
a reason so don't be afraid.

If it's meant
to be
it will
happen!

..........Mind

Keeping us down

We go to school to learn and end up
not learning much at all,

Instead we learn how to party flirt with
girls and dribble and shoot a ball,

There isn't much knowledge going to our brains,

We gain no wisdom because we're
being mentally trained,

So we can uphold the status quo,

And the wheels keep turning on this vicious cycle,

If you knew what trouble we're in you
might even go psycho,

If you're being set up to fail chances are you
might become a failure,

Being fed promises of false hope,

Were looking up from the bottom and the people up top aren't kind enough to throw us a rope,

But I say if they won't throw down the rope then lets find a ladder,

The more you climb to the top the more these images of fake illusions begin to shatter,

When your being kept down you feel non existent,

But all the anger and rage you want to let out you have to resist it,

I'm just like you because I'm starting from the bottom,

What I found out is all the answers are already within me to all my problems,

And if you dig deep enough all the questions you have you too can solve them,

We all have to stay focused and never let up,

Even if it feels like you're being kept down always try to keep your head up.

"Even

when

feeling down

keep your

head up"

"Always

stay

focused"

Ghetto greatness

Living in a place of hopelessness,

Broken dreams and forgotten memories,

Liquor stores,

And gang wars,

But people still find the strength to wake up,

People are sleep walking off of drugs and
I just wish they would wake up,

But people get high so they don't have to deal
with the harsh realities,

Not a dime in their pockets and they've never
heard of a salary,

It's so hard for a person living in the ghetto,

They should be awarded a medal,

Being there shows you the effects of the devil,

Living in a modern day concentration camp,

And yet you can still find the strength
to become a world champ,

You're going against the odds,

That must be the strength of god,

Living in the land of the lost,

But you still have the desire to become a boss,

When they placed us here they did us a favor,

Because in the long run the effects of the ghetto
can only make us greater.

"Rise
above
the odds"

Detached

Every time I write I detach from this
physical realm,

And I head to a place where only spiritual
beings dwell,

My heaven could be another man's hell,

I'm even starting to detach from this society,

I am no longer in tune with the norm,

With the thoughts that impregnate my mind
a new society will probably be born,

I'm not of this earthly dimension,

And being here everyday feels like I'm
living in prison,

So I detach to head back to my place of origin,

That place is filled with such heavenly creatures,

Pure spiritual beings with no physical bodies
or facial features,

Just pure kinetic energy,

In the physical world you could never experience
this type of synergy,

When I go to this place I never want to return,

But I come back so other people can experience
what I've learned.

Detach

from this

world!

Human being

What makes a human a being?

Is it language walking up right or
materialistic things?

What is it to be a human?

If you asked six different people you'll get
six different answers,

So is a human just a state of being,

If so are you in a state of happiness or sadness,

Joy or madness,

Are you in a state of light or blackness,

Since a human is only a state of being you can
always transition,

Because only you can control the state
in which you exist in,

Understand that you are the light and
your mind is the prism,

Knowing this will put you in a state of ecstasy,

Every conscious being is in control
of their own destiny.

What

makes us

human?

Control your

thoughts!

When the created becomes the creator.

When the created becomes the creator,

There isn't a feeling that's greater,

To watch your creation grow and blossom,

There can't be anything that feels more
awesome,

Like giving birth to a child,

And watching them grow up must really feel wild,

The universe created the cosmos then
the cosmos created galaxies,

Your brain houses your mind and your mind
creates thoughts and those thoughts create
your reality,

That must mean are minds are intergalactic,

The feeling this creates will make you
feel fantastic,

We are creators that can create one might
even call it magic,

This gift is already within us we just have
to find it,

And I decided to write this poem so everyone
could be reminded.

Learn to

become a

creator!

Thoughts....

Excuse the excuses

I've never really understood excuses,

To me they've always been pointless
and useless,

There just mental blocks that hold you back and
that's what the truth is,

People let their fears hold them back from getting
things accomplished,

Then they use their fears as an excuse on why
they can't get things accomplished,

Sometimes your mind can be your worst enemy,

That's because too many negative thoughts are
clouding your mind from past memories,

You must learn from the past and not let
it dictate your future,

Because If you don't learn from your past you're
probably going to hate your future,

With Excuses you just create for yourself
more obstacles,

If you eliminate your excuses anything
can become possible.

Whats the

point of

making

excuses?

......of a pure mind

Capture the essence

So natural and spiritual,

A blessing and a miracle,

Untouched and so pure,

When perfect harmony and balance go to war,

When great becomes greatness,

When something dead becomes alive,

When dark clouds become bright skies,

This is what occurs when you capture
your essence,

When you realize you're a miracle and
understand what you've been blessed with,

Many people have gone astray,

And if they won't capture their essence
their begin to fade away,

Their become memories of the past that won't
witness the future,

People are sick without a cure,

They may look like adults but they're still
mentally immature,

You can't just find your essence you
must capture it,

You must learn to control and master it,

When this happens life becomes more pleasant,

Much more beautiful and majestic,

So never be afraid to capture your essence.

"Learn

how to capture it"

Futuristic thoughts

My past becomes their future,

My futuristic thoughts are beyond their
comprehension,

I know what their thinking before they
even think it,

This type of mind power has always been
kept a secret,

Most people are still pondering what
I already know,

My mind just grows and grows,

My thought process is fast it's moving at turbo,

I'm going to be here forever because
my mind is eternal,

Your great grandchildren will read about me,

And your mind must still be trapped in
the past if you doubt me,

I only like to keep futuristic people around me,

So if you're not close with me that means your
mind is still stuck in the past and can't break
through the futuristic boundaries,

If you're focused on history then
you will become history,

Just a distant memory,

Futuristic thoughts give me super natural energy,

So if you want to step into the future
just depend on me.

"Make
your
thoughts
futuristic ones"

Vanishing society

The society were living in is quickly
beginning to vanish,

And anybody trying to hold on to it
will vanish with it,

A society based off of lies,

This dimension will crumble once the
truth starts to rise,

The educational system is steadily diving,

But on the other hand the prison system
is thriving,

And this is the society that we are so proud of,

A society filled with new technologies,

And college degrees,

But there's still thousands of starving children
and we can't even acknowledge their needs,

Sometimes I wonder if other people see
this or is it just me,

The thought of all this starts to disgust me,

But most people don't care if it doesn't
affect them directly,

And those same people will be the ones affected
the most when this society falls,

So ask yourself do you really care?

And if not you may be the first to disappear.

Prepare

for a new

society!

The deepest puddle

Feels like I'm drowning in the deepest puddle,

Everyday feels like the deepest struggle,

Water slowly filling up my dark lungs,

Living in dark silence only hearing my heart drum,

With no place to finish and no place to start from,

Trapped in the land of forever forgotteness,

I never thought a bad apple could become more rotten than this,

I'm breaking down physically and mentally,

Not even any change in my pocket so nothing makes sense to me,

Living this dull boring life even death seems to
be like a big event to me,

Because we all have to die eventually,

Feels like I'm locked up in the penitentiary,

People say I shouldn't let these dark
thoughts get to me,

But some things people say doesn't
mean shit to me,

They could never walk in my shoes
because they wouldn't fit you see,

Exercising my demons because my
life is out of shape,

Four walls closing in on me and I'm
looking for a way to escape,

Every moment could be a moment too late,

I just hope this deep puddle doesn't seal my fate.

"Beware of the puddle"

Reflection

Looking at myself in the mirror,

But no one is staring back because my
eyes are filled with terror,

Looking at myself because only I can
be pure with me,

And I'm seeing deep reflections of insecurities,

I'm a bright person with a dark reflection,

Guess I have to go through this to teach
my heart a lesson,

I'm falling into a dark depression,

I'm being sucked into a black hole,

With no way to exit,

My life is becoming a mess quick,

A hard life is becoming even harder,

Dark days are now becoming darker,

I have no motivation and no energy,

A mind clouded with bad memories,

Looking at myself for a solution,

But I can't think straight because my mind
is filled with pollution,

Just hope the dots in my life begin to connect,

Then maybe one day I can look back on
this and reflect.

Look into
the mirror and
ask yourself
what do you
see?

The light

There's a dim light shining on humanity,

The world seems to be very dark and filled
with insanity,

Were all trapped in the web of the spider,

Raising our levels of consciousness can make
a dim light become brighter,

Without any light people become cold
and heartless,

I want to become that bright light that
shines in the darkness,

It only takes one person to illuminate thousands,

With collective consciousness we could even
move mountains,

A bright light can make a cold soul become
quite warm,

And a bright mind can eventually turn into
a pure light form,

As human beings we create our own energy,

And it can be used to create friends or enemy's,

The first step to reaching the light is doing away
with the negative tendencies,

If your life is in a dark place don't forget that the
light is within you,

And if dark forces try to take over remember you
already have the light to defend you.

"The light

is within

you"

Life is a miracle

―――――――――

Life is but a miracle,

So beautiful and spiritual,

Intelligent and elegant,

Such wonderful embellishments,

So godly and heaven sent,

Bad thoughts become irrelevant,

I'm creating opportunities other people
may never get,

Filled with lovely endeavours,

Smart and yet still so clever,

Dark sky's can turn into tropical weather,

Life's filled with colorful creativity,

Life's always projecting prosperity,

So I can reject the fear in me,

Never again will I neglect my therapy,

Because that's what writing is to me,

It's a miracle and gift to me,

When I'm feeling down it uplifts me,

Without it no one would understand or get me,

With my writings I create miracles,

Every time my pen touches the paper
I can feel my spirit flow.

"This miracle called life is whatever you decide to make it"

"Make your decsion"

So different

I've never really cared for the political powers,

To me they've always seemed like pitiful cowards,

Preying on the weak and defenseless,

Leaving us simple minded and senseless,

And people still put their faith in them,

People go to church believing the preacher holds
the key to heaven,

So they put all their faith in the reverend,

Holding on to every word he says without asking
any questions,

I'm so different from the masses,

To me the things they do holds no logic,

They pay all this money to go to college,

To realize they never learned any real knowledge,

It's all one big scam,

Created by uncle Sam,

To keep down the working man,

We must open up are eye lids,

I'll be sure to pass this knowledge on to my kids,

Sometimes it feels like I'm the only person with sense,

But now I understand I have to be different in order to make a difference.

"Become different to make a difference"

Poetic power

_____

The potent power of poetry,

I always feel the power when new concepts
are bestowed on me,

It's an amazing sensation when the feeling
takes over me,

A hidden characteristic even my own mom
wouldn't know it's me,

It creates a realistic reality,

To keep me separated from all these
materialistic travesties,

It uplifts me to new elements of thought,

And keeps me away from all the
irrelevant thoughts,

It helps me to become even more true with me,

I'm a leader of the new school while most others
skipped out like truancy,

With this type of power the future is even
no longer new to me,

Moving in and out of the time space continuum,

So nothing in this earthly realm can
discontinue him,

So even when I'm dead and gone people
will still remember him.

Poetry is

my power

what is

yours?

Show off

———————

Political parties perpetrating perfectness,

Crippling the community by treating us like
clowns in circuses,

Lust love and loyalty,

The rush of riches and royalty,

The plush power of poetry,

Like kobe in the clutch on a scoring spree,

A lot of bitter banter boring me,

Amazing actions happen accordingly,

I'm speaking special superior spirituality,

I'm tweaking the threshold of tactical totality,

Mental murder manipulating our morality,

Rigid ruckus rockin our reality,

Fake folks fiction does not flatter me,

I'm bravely boasting my brolick benevolence,

Just to show you that my mind is
truly heaven sent.

Thoughts of
a pure mind

Thoughts of
a pure mind

Thoughts of
a pure mind

Thoughts of a pure mind

Spiritual intellect

Every time the paper and pen connect,

I release my spiritual intellect,

It's a miracle that women and men respect,

It's the purest form of intelligence,

It's not learned from other humans because
it truly is heaven sent,

The most intelligent minds wouldn't be
able to imagine it,

Not even Einstein himself would be able
to fathom it,

In my mind you could on lock the mystery
of antiquity,

In my mind I see new geometric patterns because
there is no quit in me,

My mind and the heavens are adjacent,

A superhero just wondering where his cape went,

An intergalactic being just waiting on
his spaceship,

My mind is the UFO that will release me
from this matrix,

So I can separate from all this earthly malarkey,

To truly unlock my spiritual intellect I'm now
understanding that my heart is the key.

Spiritual

intellect is

within us all!

Beautiful ugly

Life can be ugly life can be gritty,

Life can be beautiful life can be pretty

Life can be whatever you desire,

Only oxygen can unite the fire,

So every breath you take should be extraordinary,

Sometimes you must walk the path alone even if it's cold and scary,

You have to learn to accept the beautiful with the ugly,

I'm the only person that can judge me,

Life is a quest life is a journey,

Sometimes life can be very disturbing,

Waking up sometimes and I don't even
feel worthy,

It's like watching the sunshine during
a thunderstorm,

Something weird to one person could
be another persons norm,

It's all in the eye of the beholder,

This is the science of the beautiful ugly,

Something repulsive to you might
not disgust me,

Even if it's filled with poverty maybe something
could still be learned from a third world country?

Maybe they're more in tune with spirituality
instead of materialism,

Maybe their a third world country because
of imperialism,

Ever think a homeless person could be more
civilized than a person in a business suit?

Understand something that looks beautiful could really be hideous,

And something that appears ugly can be filled with prettiness.

Can you feel your mind transforming?

Your thoughts are almost becoming pure.

Keep reading!

When the inner comes outward

When the inner becomes outer,

No words because sometimes silence
speaks louder,

When inner thoughts manifest outward
into reality,

On the outside one may look like a peasant but
on the inside feel like your majesty,

When inner thoughts of a kingdom manifest one
can begin to live life lavishly,

But most people's thoughts are negative so their
thoughts manifest into travesties,

With the beauty of inner power,

This ugly world could be devoured,

There could never be peace in the world until
we find inner peace,

And manifest outward so every corner of the
world could be reached,

We all have to live our lives more heroically,

I dig deep inside my inner self and it comes
outward to you in the form of poetry.

"Dig deep

within

yourself

and bring

it outward"

F*ck the world

I say f*ck this world and all of its problems,

I say f*ck the world raw with no condemn,

To impregnate this world so it can give birth to
a new one,

The new world has to be loved and nurtured,

We neglected mother earth so she became filled
with hate and torture,

Mother earth will then give birth to a daughter,

The old world was a bastard child the new world
needs the love her father,

A new world will give birth to a new civilization,

And a new civilization will give birth to
a new society,

And that will lead to the birth of a new mentality,

A mind that is pure and not tainted
with corruption,

The canvas of our minds are now painted with
destruction

Now we think hate is more prominent than love,

But there can never be anything more dominant
than love,

The old world was born then hated,

The new world must be loved but first the old
world must be fornicated.

A new

world must be born!

Thoughts of

a pure mind

Thoughts of

a pure mind

Thoughts of

a pure

mind

Thoughts..........

Open your eye'(s)

Open up your eye,

Not the two on your face but the
one in your mind,

The all seeing eye that helps you see
through the illusions,

Then no longer will you live life in confusion,

Then you'll be able to see what others
can't witness,

You'll begin to attain a whole new concept
of vision,

You'll begin to enter new realms and dimensions,

A positive role model might start to look
like a negative criminal,

This is what occurs when the power of the third
eye reaches its pinnacle,

When something appears it's being done
for a good cause the story behind it might
be a little more cynical,

The number one thing that closes the
third eye is fear,

So only believe half of what you see and
none of what you hear.

Keep

your

eye(s)

open!

Without my spirit

Me without my spirit,

Is like a rabbit with no carrot,

A wedding ring without marriage,

A lie without truth,

A house with no roof,

A basketball player with no hoop,

The sun without the moon,

A fork without the spoon,

A musical note without the tune,

A bride without the groom,

Happiness without a smile,

A mom without her child,

Egypt Without the Nile,

A war without the battle,

A judge without a gavel,

A boat without a paddle,

What I'm trying to say is I could never
be without my spirit,

It's something within me that I will
always cherish.

"Thoughts of a pure mind teaching you to find your spirit"

It's within us all!

Magic

Writing for me has always been so practical,

Every time I write the sensation I get feels
so magical,

Its like I'm a wizard and my pen is the wand,

My spirit and my mind are an unbreakable bond,

Like electron and protons,

Without either one my life would be so gone,

When the sky turns grey and life feels so tragic,

All I have to do is take out my wand
and release my magic,

I'm a magician,

My mind is a prism,

Transferring the light to make a colorful vision,

We all have magic within us you just
have to believe it,

And when this occurs even a blind
person could see it.

"We all

have magic

within us

you just

have to believe"

Freedom

———————

They call it freedom because if you think
anything is free then you must be dumb,

This world we live in I will never understand it,

We even have to pay for things that are found
naturally on the planet,

Elements like water and oil that have been here
since the beginning of time,

Then they promote love to sell jewelry while little
kids work for hours in diamond mines,

Most people are blind to the facts,

Their minds in a trap,

Watching out for snakes in the grass
with no spines in their backs,

Some people look like humans but have
very in humane qualities,

We have to open our minds and think more
logically,

If you want freedom chances are you're
going to become poor,

Because freedom is something we
all have to pay for.

What

kind of

freedom

are you

searching for?

Pharaoh

———————

I think I'm a pharaoh,

But I just gave up the gold and jewelry
for today's modern apparel,

Now I've come back to the world reincarnated,

I'm one of god's favorites,

The world is dying and I've been sent
here to save it,

But sometimes I just rather save myself,

I've made mistakes in the past and I still
haven't forgave myself,

I've given away my crown to live amongst
the people,

And what I've noticed is the world is in need
of a huge upheaval,

As you can see my minds prolific,

This is a poem that I've translated from the
hieroglyphics,

This would explain why my minds so different,

I'm here for a cause and it's very real
and specific.

An ancient

deity has

now been reborn

To uplift the masses!

Dear God

Dear God I'm dreaming of heaven but
I'm stuck in hell,

It's hard to trust others when I don't
even trust myself,

It's hard to love others when I don't
even love myself,

God I need you to touch down and put
your hands on me,

My imagination is filled with suicidal fantasies,

But I try to not let it show guess it's just
the man in me,

This is full blown insanity,

This torture and torment you must know
I'm hating this,

I can't take it anymore I'm even starting
to become an atheist,

Even with my head down I keep walking,

I never cared about what the preacher
was talking,

Because I'd much rather talk to you one on one,

You're my father and I'm your son,

Wondering how I haven't drowned in my sleep
from all the tears at night I'm crying,

Wondering if there's more happiness in dying,

Then I'll be away from all the misery
and depression,

God let my spirit free and my days of being
trapped in this flesh end.

God can you hear me?

Alternate universe

_____

What if Barack Obama wasn't the first black
president,

What if political parties weren't donkeys
and elephants,

What if the political parties weren't even relevant,

Imagine if Einstein was an athlete and Michael
Jordan was a scientist,

What if most of the worlds knowledge came from
ancient Egyptian papyrus,

What if Martin Luther King was more like Adolf,

And was just a political pawn that was payed off,

What if summer felt like winter and winter
felt like summer,

What if zero was the most important number,

What if sleeping wasn't needed and
we didn't have to slumber,

What if we could speak to each other
telepathically,

What if we could learn trigonometry
math at three,

What if we used 100% of our brain power,

What if the clock ticked sixty minutes and
it was still the same hour,

What if the European renaissance was
started by the Moors,

This is a look into my universe and I'm
bringing it into yours.

"Your entering the
new universe"

The

journey is

almost over.

How do

you feel?

Have the thoughts

in your mind

changed?

Universe or 1verse

Protons and neutrons orbit the nucleus
of an atom,

The same way planets orbit a sun,

Me and the universe one in the same,

Uni means one and I'm one man with one mind
and one brain,

So can the universe be explained in one verse,

When I die there will be one funeral one church
and one hearse,

So even in death me and the universe are still
inseparable,

Universal consciousness has a grip on me
and it can't let go,

Was the universe created or did it always exist,

Was I created or did my conscious always exist,

These are two questions that I want answered on
my very long list,

Because I feel as if I've been here forever,

And every life time my mind becomes
more pure and clever,

Being here for so long you'll become
overwhelmed with frustration,

This lifetime I'm making sure my mission
is fulfilled so this becomes my last incarnation.

Is there only one universe?

Thoughts of a pure mind

Thoughts of a pure mind

Thoughts of a pure mind

Drunken soberness

So many days of drunken soberness,

I swear to God I'm so over this,

With no alcohol in my system and
I still feel intoxicated,

Everyday it feels like I'm boxing Satan,

It's like I can't escape and I'm boxed
in the matrix,

Life is becoming very ugly and she
needs a facelift,

Life is walking dead in my direction but
I'm too afraid to face it,

So I've decided to turn my back on it,

So drunk now that my vision turns black
and I begin to vomit,

Feels like my mind is so outer space and it's
soaring on a comet,

I don't really care what anyone thinks so there's
no need to comment,

The girl that I love doesn't even understand how
much I really love her,

I just want her to know that God is the only
one I put above her,

And If she reads this I want her to know I just
want to romance you,

And kiss you like the people in France do,

But that's only If you're willing and give
me the chance to.

Have you ever felt drunken soberness?

Harmony

When everything is working in perfect harmony,

There's no dark thoughts harming me,

It lights a spark in me,

Its like my heart is free,

And no longer caged in,

I no longer feel like a strange man,

A confused soul begins to understand God's
game plan,

And finds a path for himself in this strange land,

I feel like a changed man,

But on the outside I still look like the same man,

That's because perfect harmony is something
that occurs within you,

It's the beginning of inner peace,

And the ending of the inner beast,

I call it spiritual homeostasis,

It eliminates all the phony craziness,

It could change the mind of an atheist,

Being in perfect harmony will take you
to ecstasy,

Releasing your spirit and now from
the flesh you're free.

"Were all

searching

for perfect harmony"

Who am I ?

Guess I'm on a quest to find out who I really am,

Am I a spiritual being or just a common man?

Am I what society thinks of me?

Should I base the concept of myself on how
society views me?

Or should I just not care and follow my heart
to become the true me?

I'm sick of living this fake facade,

Searching and searching for a place with God,

Guess i've been searching in the wrong places,

Looking in the mirror and I seem so faceless,

If you know me then you'd call me calvin but i'm
not really sure what my name is,

It's not a name that I chose because
it was given to me,

By my parents but they would've named me
something different if they really knew me,

But how can they know me when I'm
still trying to find myself,

It feels like this whole time i've been hiding
from myself,

I think it's about time I uplift my true
self out of the darkness,

I'm starting to realize what I am and thats pure
consciousness.

Who

are you?

Yes or No

Does he make you feel special?

Or does he bring you headaches and stress you?

Does he make you proud and uplift you?

Does he even bother to understand or get you?

Does he respect you for your mind and spirit?

Does he make you feel like a women
being cherished?

Maybe you should ask yourself these questions
to know if he's the one you should be with,

If you answered no to most of these questions
maybe you never knew how a lady should
be treated,

Since you never knew you accepted the
unacceptable,

If he doesn't answer yes to most of these
questions maybe it's time to let him go?

And there will be a man that will answer
yes to these questions and all he needs
is an opportunity,

You just have to follow your heart and keep a
sharp mind and keep the two working in unity.

Yes

or

No

In her arms

_____

It feels so heavenly when i'm in her arms,

It's like nothing can hurt me and
I can't be harmed,

She holds me as if she never wants to let me go,

Every time she leaves my side I can see
it crushing her soul,

And I never want her to let me go,

When she leaves my side it also
crushes my soul,

Thats why I always tell her to hold me tighter,

When i'm in her arms a dark day becomes
brighter,

Us being together is the perfect dream to me,

I don't think she understands how much she
truly means to me,

The thought of living a life without her is
too painful to imagine,

It's something I truly hope never happens,

I'll always be truthful because I don't
want to lie to her,

This is much deeper than puppy love because
i'm even willing to die for her,

If sacrificing my life would give her a better life,

I never want to cause her harm,

These are the feelings and thoughts I get when
i'm in her arms.

It's a great feeling to feel!

Hope you enjoyed the book and opened your mind to new ways of thinking. I really enjoyed writing this book and bringing it to you. After reading this book it becomes yours and apart of your essence. So don't look at this book as just something to read look at it as something that has become a part of you. As you can see the last couple of pages are blank. Why are they blank you ask? There blank because I really want you to make this book apart of you. So with the blank pages you can write your own poetry, make your own drawings or whatever your heart desires. So go ahead and make this book yours!

Yours truly:

Calvin Bland

Follow me
on twitter @ablandboy1

And check out
my other poetry book
Stories From A
Bland Boy
at amazon.com

www.ingramcontent.com/pod-product-compliance
Lightning Source LLC
Chambersburg PA
CBHW060524030426

42337CB00015B/1986